LEAD
WITH
MERCY

THE BUSINESS CASE
FOR COMPASSION

ROBERT GOODSON

Lead With Mercy Publishing

Lead with Mercy
The Business Case for Compassion
All Rights Reserved.
Copyright © 2015 Robert Goodson
v2.0

Cover Photo © 2015 thinkstockphotos.com. All rights reserved - used with permission.

Lead With Mercy Publishing

ISBN: 978-0-578-15277-6

Library of Congress Control Number: 2015900914

PRINTED IN THE UNITED STATES OF AMERICA

TABLE OF CONTENTS

PRAISE FOR
LEAD WITH MERCY

"In a world where patience and understanding are sometimes in short supply, we could all use a little mercy. Leaders will benefit from answering the questions raised in this book."

Randal D. Fullhart, Commandant of Cadets, Virginia Tech

"Warren Bennis once said, 'While managers know how to do things right, leaders know how to do the right thing.' *Lead with Mercy* brings new meaning to these words and offers business leaders a True North to navigate the morally murky waters of today with the timeless principles of yesterday. The book will serve as a touchstone text for generations of leaders seeking a higher purpose in their work."

Dr. Jeffrey Kuhn, Founder and CEO, GrowthLeaders®

"*Lead with Mercy* is an excellent book which addresses the timely issue of corporate leadership, especially in our tough and sluggish economic times. Rob's use of his own military and business experiences truly resonates with the reader because most of us have been in similar situations. Rob's book is also one of the few I have read that was courageous enough to tackle the discussion of how to manage the corporate responsibility of business leaders to make a profit while also staying true to their spiritual compass. Not only does Rob's argument show that a strong spiritual grounding and merciful leadership are compatible with difficult business decisions, but he proves that they actually have a great return on investment. If for no other reason than this last point, every entrepreneur should read *Lead with Mercy* to help them establish a foundation they can build their company upon."

Jeremy Nalley, Owner, Nalley Consulting

"Wow! What a timely and important book. Rob promises to make a business case for compassion in leadership, and he succeeds. Using a variety of examples and his insurmountable logic, he shows how leaders can improve results while leading from the heart. Skeptical? Perfect. Rob is ready for every objection you can throw his way, and will show you how having compassion as a leader will create a more engaged and responsible workforce, build a stronger organization, and take your career to the next level – without sacrificing practical, analytical decision-making or a focus on performance and discipline. This book is an invaluable guide to being a more flexible leader capable of leading the most complex organizations in volatile times. Prepare to be challenged and inspired."

Andrew Neitlich, Founder and Director,
Center for Executive Coaching

"Rob's exceptional ability to weave together his military, business, and spiritual knowledge and experiences truly makes the intangible idea of merciful leadership tangible, alive, and very real. His business case for leading with mercy is actually a call to action. As he writes with both passion and humility, the reader is left with one very important question: How can I be a better leader by being a merciful leader? Read the book now and change the course of whatever organization you lead now and in the future. It's that good."

Todd Uterstaedt, President & CEO, Baker & Daboll, LLC;
and Co-Founder, *Daughters in Charge*

"All leaders in all sectors – corporate, non-profit, government – have the opportunity to contribute significantly to the lives of those who follow them. Leaders have the opportunity to support, mentor, educate and inspire. And whether we realize it or not, being compassionate and leading with mercy is not only good for those we lead, it is good for our mission and good for the bottom line of our organization. In *Lead with Mercy*, Rob uses humor and compelling examples to make the business case – and more importantly, the moral case – for adopting an approach that can enrich the lives of those leaders who adopt it as well as those who look to them for guidance and direction."

Barbara Van Dahlen, Ph.D., Founder & President, *Give an Hour*;
TIME Magazine 2012 "100 Most Influential People in the World"

INTRODUCTION

The idea for this book first took root as I was driving from Sarasota to Tampa, Florida in the spring of 2014. I was on the way to the airport to catch a flight home to Virginia, having just completed a thought-provoking seminar on executive coaching, led by Andrew Neitlich, of the Center for Executive Coaching. As I drove I listened to *The Catholic Channel* on satellite radio and the commentators were discussing a conflict within the family of one of the speakers. The speaker, Jennifer Fulwiler, said to the other commentator (a priest named Father Jonathon Morris) something to the effect of "I tried to lead with mercy." I found that statement to be very powerful and compelling … what a great name for a blog or a newsletter … or a book, I thought. Out of curiosity I searched the web for the phrase. The first two references were to Pope Francis (including a video posted by the same Father Morris I just mentioned). The third was the score of the Mercy (a school name) tennis match. Interesting but not really remarkable, I thought (although I am a big Pope Francis fan) and didn't think much else of it.

The phrase kept creeping into my mind at work, though, which seemed a bit odd. As a sinner, I (try to) thank the Lord for His mercy every day … but that's faith, not business, I told myself. As a parent,

I (generally) show mercy to my children ... but that's parenthood, not business, I said. As an executive in a Fortune 500 company, mercy is not generally in my daily vernacular of profit, revenue, and billable hours ... that's business, and not a place for the faint of heart looking for mercy and compassion.

But perhaps it should be a part of business ... maybe even the foundation of it. I can hear the collective cringe of C-suite executives, hard-core MBA students, and executive coaches everywhere – great, another feel-good, theoretical book about leadership, with a dash of religious undertone. Even my wife, who believes strongly in mercy and a business professional herself, said to me, "What the heck is leading with mercy ... I thought you were going to write about something useful?"

Guilty as charged. It's my sincere hope that this book will make you feel good. There's not a whole lot of theory, but the theory that's here is backed up by research and observations from experts and executives much more intelligent and successful than I am. Yes, this book is about leadership. Not just leadership theory, but the leadership that I have studied, been subject to, and executed (not always well) in over 20 years as a cadet and student, soldier, manager, coach, and executive. As for the religious undertone, I'm not judging you, and pray you will do the same in return (see what I did there?). Besides, I've offered many respected secular sources for my assertions.

In this short book I will lay out a framework – the how – to leading with mercy. Within a framework of leading with mercy (Figure 1), there are five major elements: defining mercy, earning the right to lead, responsibility, clarity of vision, and leading from the heart.

Figure 1. Lead With Mercy Framework.

Defining ⓜercy

ⓔarn the Right to Lead

ⓡesponsibility

ⓒlarity of Vision

Lead From ⓨour Heart

❖ *Defining Mercy* sets the stage for why compassion has a place in business and leadership

❖ *Earning the right to lead* is as straightforward as leading by example and the golden rule.

❖ *Responsibility* is about accountability of the leader and the led.

❖ *Clarity of vision* is about inspiring others to new possibilities.

❖ *Leading with your heart* is about motivating, recognizing, and celebrating excellence.

In the following chapters we will talk about each of these five elements and then – for the readers who prefer to lead from the head (not that leading from the head and heart are mutually exclusive, quite the opposite) – end with a discussion of the business case for leading with mercy. At the end of chapters two through five, I will provide some questions you could ask of yourself or someone you might be coaching or mentoring to lead with mercy. While this is a serious and impactful topic, I will keep it lighthearted. It is not my intent to preach; rather, I hope to share my thoughts and perspectives. By the end, it is my hope you will agree there is indeed a place for mercy and compassion in business; *and not only is there a place for such leadership, but that it can lead to a successful, profitable business.*

And so, with a little nudging from my wife (despite her misgivings on the topic), I decided to write this book. My hope is you'll stick with me until the end and that I convince you of the business case for leading with mercy. If it's a decent book, then the credit goes to those that inspired the lessons within it. If it's bad, then the responsibility is all mine … so please be merciful.

- Rob Goodson

P.S. I'd love to hear your thoughts and perspectives on leadership. Please visit me at: *www.leadwithmercy.com*

CHAPTER ONE

DEFINING MERCY

---

*Of all the management principles I have adopted over
the years ... there is one I aspire to live by more than
any other ... managing compassionately.*
– Jeff Weiner, CEO of LinkedIn

What is mercy? As I read several definitions of the word, I came
upon one in *Webster's* that seemed apropos for a book about leadership and business: "Compassion or forbearance shown especially to
an offender or to one subject to one's power." It is the part about
showing compassion to someone who is subject to your power
that intrigues me. It is intriguing because it is a deliberate choice.
Nothing is forcing the person in power to show mercy to the person
subject to his power. So why do it?

I am already convinced of the power of mercy. It is a central
teaching of the Christian church and many other world religions and
spiritual beliefs. Even the most secular of us would not be surprised

to hear of references to mercy in the major monotheistic religions such as Christianity, Judaism, and Islam. You do not have to search hard to find references to compassion or *karuna,* in religions and belief systems such as Buddhism and Hinduism either.[1] So in the context of the spiritual or eternal salvation, mercy is quite common and quite welcome by many. In fact, I had a tough time finding references to the word mercy (they all seem to prefer compassion) in a context that was not religious, spiritual, or philosophical.

The world of business, however, is not about salvation ... it is about the bottom line, and soft, intangible concepts like mercy, compassion, patience, and forgiveness do not really have a logical place in business. In a 24/7 global business cycle, leaders do not have time for forgiveness – they are being held accountable for results, not compassion, by boards, customers, investors, and other stakeholders. Right? Or is there a place for mercy, and should we as leaders make time to show it?

As you have likely surmised by now, there is a compelling case for mercy in the world of business, and especially amongst the leaders of business. It is especially important for leaders, because we set the tone for culture and behavior in our organizations.

The case for leading with mercy is made even more compelling when you consider the common traits or characteristics often found in successful leaders. These characteristics do not guarantee successful leadership, nor are they found in all successful leaders. A significant body of research as summarized in Bruce Peltier's *The Psychology of Executive Coaching,* however, concludes that many successful leaders bear these traits which I associate to leading with mercy. These relevant traits of successful leaders include:

❖ *Integrity:* If I were asked to pick one trait closely associated with merciful leadership, I would choose integrity. From leading by example, delegating responsibility, to encouraging risk taking ... the foundation is trust in the leader.

❖ *Emotional maturity:* While this trait has broad meaning, the component that I associate with mercy is the ability to "care about others" and empathize.

❖ *Vision:* The capacity of a leader for organizational vision and articulating that vision is a common trait amongst successful leaders ... and as we will discuss, clarity of vision is a key component of the *Lead with Mercy* framework.[2]

While many of my examples come from for-profit business, the benefits of leading with mercy apply to many organizations (government, military, non-profit, religious, and businesses large and small). This is more than a feel-good story; in fact, it is a case that rates against more popular business-minded notions like efficiency, incentives, and optimization – which at their core are all about making or keeping more money. Phrases like *compassionate management, managing compassionately,* and *conscious capitalism* are rolling off the tongues of chief executives like LinkedIn's, Jeff Weiner, and the blogs of leading business magazines like *Harvard Business Review.*[3][4][5] The former CEO of PUMA (an international sportswear brand), Jochen Zeitz – who turned around a corporation near bankruptcy – believes a leader's job is "to exercise authority with the greatest possible understanding and circumspection."[6]

So am I saying that leading with mercy has true return on investment, or ROI? Yes, I am. In fact, I am saying the ROI can be quite significant because the monetary investment is nominal at best and the return can be substantial – both the tangible and intangible return. In order to realize this significant ROI, we have to lead our people; and before we can lead successfully, we have to earn the right to lead.

CHAPTER TWO

EARNING THE RIGHT TO LEAD: THE GOLDEN RULE

---

*In everything, therefore, treat people the
same way you want them to treat you.*
– Matthew 7:12

One of the perennial arguments in the intellectual study of leadership is whether leadership ability is something with which you are born – the natural leader – or something you learn through experience. I do not claim to know the answer; I suspect it is a little or a lot of both, depending on the individual. What I do feel confident in saying is that while you may be given the authority to lead, no one can be given the right to lead. You have to earn it.

When I was commissioned as a second lieutenant in the United States Army from the Virginia Tech Army ROTC program, I outranked every enlisted person in the U.S. Armed Forces from the brand-new private or airman to the most senior command sergeant major or master chief petty officer. That group of enlisted service members included (much to my joy) my father, an army sergeant major at the time I was commissioned. He gave me my first salute on the Upper Quad (the home of the Virginia Tech Corps of Cadets), a tradition for newly commissioned military officers. The salute is an outward sign of respect and implies subordination. By virtue of my commission, I was given the authority to lead. I felt pretty powerful that beautiful day in Blacksburg, Virginia. I suspect many of you, especially the military veterans, have some inkling of the rest of the story.

As the son of an enlisted man, I had a sneak preview of the relationship between officers and enlisted soldiers, especially that of junior officers and more senior enlisted soldiers, known as non-commissioned officers. It helped me avoid at least some of the rookie mistakes of thinking I was in charge merely by virtue of my authority. At almost every echelon of the military there is an officer in charge, along with a non-commissioned officer who serves alongside that officer. For example, in the army a platoon leader has a platoon sergeant, and a company commander has a first sergeant. In many cases, the non-commissioned officer has significant tenure (or time in service) compared to the officer. For example, when I was a company commander I had been in the army five years; my first sergeant was pushing twenty years. I will not bore you with the rest of the story, but needless to say, I had to earn the right to lead "my" non-commissioned officer as well as all the soldiers under my command. By regulation they had to follow orders, but not until I earned their respect would they grant me the right to lead. What I found was that in putting in the time and effort to earn the right to lead, I learned an awful lot about myself – my strengths, my weaknesses, and my preconceptions – all of which made me a better leader (and a better person).

While the situation is somewhat different in the business world, we still have to earn the right to lead. I argue it may even be a little more difficult in the world of business to earn that right. In the military, the leader has explicit legal authority to give orders; he or she wears a uniform with insignia that clearly establishes the superior and subordinate person in a professional relationship; and the consequences of not following the leader can impact life and death (not as a penalty, but as the consequence of second-guessing, especially in a dangerous situation). So in the framework of leading with mercy, how can you earn the right to lead?

Lead by Example

From basic military training to MBA programs, we have heard the mantra of "lead by example" time and time again. Yet time and time again we see leaders of military, government, and business organizations fail at it. The reasons for that are beyond my intellect and the scope of this book. I can guess the reasons have to do with anything from inexperience, to arrogance, to apathy. What is in the scope of this book is a discussion of leading by example in the framework of leading with mercy.

One of my least-favorite phrases in professional life is: "It's not personal, it's just business." It is a trite phrase offered – sometimes with good intent – as justification for a decision that has a direct impact on someone's life (and not just their professional life), such as terminating employment. If a person is involved, it is by definition personal. This is more than a semantic argument. It is at the essence of why we should lead with mercy and compassion. I am not arguing that difficult decisions affecting people's livelihood are not necessary in business – they are unfortunately unavoidable in some cases, and I have had to make them myself. They are, however, no less personal even if necessary. So if it is unavoidable, how can we lead with mercy in this situation? How would you like to be treated in this situation?

If we stay with our scenario of terminating employment (let us say termination as a result of downsizing, as opposed to poor performance), leaders should ask themselves if they are truly leading by example. For instance, are senior leaders in the organization getting substantial raises and bonuses while cutting costs (including people)? Are senior leaders reducing the cost of executive perquisites and other controllable costs (such as excessive business meals or travel expenses)? Is the organization top-heavy (are we retaining leaders and managers at the cost of other team members – who often generate more revenue than management, especially in a professional services environment)? There are many questions a leader can and should pose in this scenario. Answering the questions appropriately (appropriate meaning the senior leaders are also feeling the pain of cost-cutting) is a way to lead with the example of mercy or compassion.

The former PUMA CEO, Jochen Zeitz, has a perspective on leading by example that I had not heard before. He suggests that "those who are good by nature will follow" the leader who sets a positive example and "those who have a rather negative character will be drawn along by the stream" of the good colleagues following the leader's example. Furthermore, leading by example inspires people to perform well.[7] In my experience, the power of leading by example should not be underestimated. For example, I once listened to a senior executive field a question from a concerned employee about his (the employee's) salary. It was a group setting. The employee was lamenting they had not received a raise that year. The senior executive responded very sympathetically and sincerely, and added something to the effect of, "I know how you feel, I took a 12 percent cut this year." The room was silent. The point was clear: The most senior leaders of the organization were sharing in the pain of declining sales and profit. Quite frankly, that particular moment made discussions with my people about no raises more bearable. I did not enjoy sharing that kind of news, but it was more palatable for me (and hopefully the recipient of the news) knowing that the leaders of our organization were leading by example and sharing in the pain of a declining market.

Virginia Tech head football coach Frank Beamer is another example of a merciful leader in a demanding business. Full disclosure: I am a bit of a Virginia Tech football fanatic and was happy to find this excuse to mention Coach Beamer and Hokie football. His leadership style and actions are relevant here, however, because as the head coach of a major college football program he faces challenges similar to other organizational leaders: managing high performers in a competitive environment, attracting and retaining talent, delivering results, and generating income, among others. Jeff Snook, the writer who assisted Beamer with his autobiography, writes that Beamer "balances the competiveness it takes to succeed with a non-existent ego and heart made of gold." Beamer's loyalty to his staff is fairly common knowledge amongst the Virginia Tech fan base. At times he has been criticized for being too loyal (this is also relevant to leading with mercy – we will talk later about tough love within the Mercy Framework). Regardless, he leads by example and shares in the pain of organizational challenges. In his autobiography he talks about taking lower salary so that his assistants' (i.e. those under his authority) salaries are competitive and they are "compensated fairly."[8]

As we discovered in Chapter One, a definition of mercy is compassion toward those who are under your authority. You do not have to show them mercy, and most of your stakeholders likely would not fault you for reducing numbers on your payroll. Consider, however, an unattributed quote the makes the point better than I can: "Choice is not about what you *can* do, it's about what you *should* do." Andreas Widmer, in his book, *The Pope and the CEO*, calls not doing what you ought even if you can justify it, consequentialism. The ends justify the means – my company was losing money, I need to cut costs, and a way to do that is to reduce the number of people you have to pay.[9] But are there ways to lead with mercy in such situations? Again, leading with mercy is not about avoiding difficult business decisions. Rather it is about leading by example and compassion – are you as a leader sharing the pain, or spreading the wealth with your colleagues?

To be sure, there are wonderful examples of companies that lead with mercy. Many companies allow for leave or vacation donation for a fellow employee who is undergoing a difficult personal situation, such as the death or sickness of a family member, and has

used up all his or her accrued paid time off. Others provide free resources (at least free to the employee), such as counseling or career
transition services, through employee assistance programs. I am
not naïve enough to think there are not business reasons for such
programs, such as retention, or attracting talent by matching competitor benefits – but looking through a positive lens, the programs
are compassionate and represent a discretionary cost (the company
chose to pay for the benefit). Additionally, leading with mercy is not
limited to major benefits and expensive programs. Many companies
allow team members to expense costs like sending flowers for a new
baby, or donations to a cause in memory of someone who has passed
away. Perhaps even more than major programs, these acts of compassion represent leading by example, for they are simple yet sincere
acts. One of my most treasured mementos from work is a simple
hand-written note from a senior partner in my firm. The partner
thanked me for my leadership during a difficult time for my team.
The story behind the note is an example of leading with mercy that
I witnessed in my own professional life.

As part of my business portfolio in a professional services firm, I
led a team of over eighty people that provided a cutting-edge service
to our client. Unfortunately the client, as was the case with many at
the time, had its budget significantly reduced, and the mission my
team supported was eliminated. With little notice my team would
go from "fully billable" (a significant metric of efficiency and productivity in our business) to zero in a matter of two weeks. In the
professional services industry it is not unusual to give team members notice of termination in such a situation. My team expected
it. I was fortunate, though, to work for a very compassionate management team. The more cynical argued it was merely an effort to

retain talent and a competitive edge. While there is some truth to that (and it makes good business sense), the team went above and beyond the standard practice in this case. Besides, leading with mercy and good business practices do not have to be mutually exclusive. My manager went to our senior partner and asked for money to cover our staff for a period of time beyond the normal notification time they would receive, before we terminated their employment. These additional weeks quite literally bought us time in which we could place people internally on other jobs or give our people time to find new employment externally while eliminating or reducing a gap in pay and benefits for them, and in many cases their families. In the end we placed about eighty percent of the team internally. And in a testament to the power of mercy and compassion, several colleagues who had necessarily taken jobs outside our company returned several months later when new opportunities arose within our team.

In his book *Search Inside Yourself: The Unexpected Path to Achieving Success, Happiness (and World Peace)*, Chade-Meng Tan cites a similar example of leading by mercy and the positive, tangible results. General Electric (GE) and a competitor both made a decision to close a plant. GE provided its employees two years' notice and external job search assistance. The competitor provided a week's notice and no job placement assistance. In a survey about a year later, the majority of former GE employees rated GE as a good place to work and 93 percent "lauded" the job placement assistance. Only three percent of the competitor's former employees noted their previous company as a good place to work.[10] OK, that is a nice story, but what is the business impact? All of these happy and unhappy former employees are potentially future customers, clients, or return employees. Each has a professional network with some level of influence, and each will propagate their positive or negative perception of their former employers. These perceptions influence professional brand and reputation, which influences whether people will use a business' products or seek a job with that business.

Lead with Integrity

Demonstrating integrity in your actions as a business leader is a critical component of leading by example; hence I have given it space as a separate section in this chapter. It is such a vital and powerful part of leadership because it is one of those rare things over which we as individuals have absolute control. If you do not lead with honesty, you have no one to blame but yourself...and your people will blame no else but you. No one can make you be untruthful or deceitful. You have a choice, and that choice illustrates volumes about you in the eyes of the people you are leading. And as I quoted earlier, choice is about doing what is right...not about what is convenient or comfortable.

While leading with integrity may not alone earn you the right to lead in the eyes of those you lead, leading without it is a surefire way to lose people's respect. My intent, however, is not to lecture about the evils of dishonesty. Rather, I hope to make the case that leading with integrity and mercy are mutually reinforcing and good for you as the leader, your people, and your company's performance.

In their book *Lift: Becoming a Positive Force in Any Situation*, Ryan and Robert Quinn write about the "influence of an other-focused state." As the name implies, being other-focused is being concerned about the impact of any given situation on others. In other words, the emphasis is less on how I feel or how a situation impacts me, but rather, how does it impact others and how do they feel about it? Backed up by academic research, the Quinns argue that by creating an environment of integrity, trust, and empathy (or mercy and compassion, in my words) you can increase people's performance because they feel valued and secure enough to try harder, take reasonable risks, and consider new solutions to challenges. Leading with integrity is an example of how good leadership influences others to act with integrity also. In a high- performance business environment, people may feel pressure to compromise their integrity in order to make their numbers or hide a deficiency in the business. If they witness the leader, however, acting with integrity and compassion even in a difficult circumstance, they will feel more secure to take the risk of telling the truth, even if it is not good news.[11]

To underscore the need to lead with integrity even further, the Quinns share the story of an experiment by Stanley Milgram designed to question why people act in ways that are inconsistent with their values. In this case the specific value was that of compassion. The experiment consisted of a person of authority (the person leading the experiment) and two subjects, a witting student and an unwitting teacher. The teacher was instructed to shock the student every time he gave the wrong answer to a question (the student did not receive an actual electric shock, but the teacher did not know this). Sixty-five percent of the time the teacher kept shocking the student despite what he thought was an increasing amount of voltage and pain to the student. The relevant lesson in the context of leading with integrity and mercy is that most people are taught from an early age to obey people in positions of authority and that tendency to obey "is strong enough to overwhelm other values, even to the point of harming our fellow human beings."[12] Jerry Burger conducted a study in 2009 based on Milgram's original study of the 1960s; his experiment had very similar results, namely people are susceptible to influence especially by authority figures (e.g. leaders).[13] So consider the implications to individuals and organizations of a leader who does not lead with integrity and mercy. Just like children assume it is acceptable to do what they see adults doing, the people you lead are likely to mimic what they assume the leader condones, implicitly or explicitly. If the leader treats people poorly or is dishonest in dealings with colleagues, customers, and stakeholders, we can expect that those he leads will do the same.

Meng from Google also writes about the power of trust in business. He notes that it "brings out the best in people" and that one way to establish trust is to lead with mercy (Meng uses the word empathy). Meng notes from his research that "key thinkers on effectiveness at work have trust as the foundation of their practices and approaches." For example, executive coach Marc Lesser, believes an effective coaching engagement starts with establishing trust. Patrick Lencioni, well-known in executive coaching and leadership development circles, offers that the number one (of five) "dysfunctions of a team" is the "absence of trust."[14]

Ethan Schutz, President and CEO of The Schutz Company*, underscores the power of trust in business and ties it (or lack thereof) to the bottom line: Schutz notes that lack of trust leads to inefficient and counterproductive activities like "conflict, malicious compliance, avoidance, and other non-productive behaviors." He goes on

---

* The Schutz Company is a consulting company; their work is grounded in Will Schutz's theory of interpersonal relations called Fundamental Interpersonal Relations Orientation (FIRO).

to note that this inefficiency results in time lost, which equates to opportunities lost.[15] The late founder of The Schutz Company, Will Schutz, claimed: "Truth telling is probably the single most cost-effective and simplest way to make major leaps in organizational productivity and worker satisfaction."[16] The implication for today's businesses, especially professional services and other knowledge-based organizations, is clear: lost time (due to lack of trust among people) equals lost money.

In the framework of leading with mercy, the power and influence of leading with integrity, or not, requires the leader to ask several introspective questions. Am I truthful in my interactions with customers, board members, investors, colleagues, and other stake-holders? Do I lead with mercy – in other words, do I consider the feelings of and impact on others and not just my own feelings and concerns? Do I hold other leaders accountable for being deceitful?

Questions to consider about earning the right to lead

1. How can I better exemplify the standards of my organization?

2. How do I as a leader share the pain of difficult decisions like downsizing?

3. How do I treat those that place their confidence in my leadership?

4. How do I consider the impact of my decisions upon others?

5. How can I better lead with integrity?

CHAPTER THREE

RESPONSIBILITY: CAST NO STONES

---

*I have always found that mercy bears
richer fruits than strict justice.*
–Abraham Lincoln

If you have read this far, you are likely at least intrigued by the notion of mercy in business or other organizational leadership. Yet even if you are buying into this notion, you are likely a bit concerned about the potential lack of accountability in a leadership framework that has as its essence mercy, compassion, generosity, or similar notions. If you are a leader in a business environment that is all about results such as revenue, margins, and shareholder value, you are wondering how in the world this author is still employed or in business (to allay those concerns, I am still employed and by at least a few accounts successful).

Leading with mercy does not mean we are not accountable as leaders, or that we cannot and should not hold those we lead responsible for their actions and results. In fact, you are not likely to find a lot of business literature that advocates letting people do as they will, with no consequences for action or inaction. So what does responsibility mean in the framework of leading with mercy? Hold that thought. Since I have used the terms responsibility and accountability somewhat interchangeably, let me first offer a distinction made by Scott Eblin in his book *The Next Level: What Insiders Know About Executive Success.*

Responsibility vs. Accountability

Eblin writes about executives needing to "pick up accountability for many results" and letting go "of responsibility for a few results." If you are responsible for something, you are the person doing the work or closely overseeing the work of others. If you are overseeing, then you are likely still stepping in at certain points to do some of the work. In short, if you are responsible, you are very personally involved, and Eblin argues that in such a case you can successfully manage only a few results at a time. The distinction is not made to claim that responsibility is bad and accountability is good. Clearly, organizations need people who are responsible and those that are accountable. This distinction, however, is quite important for a leader who aspires to even greater leadership positions.[17]

In contrast, a leader who is accountable has to answer for the results of the people that are responsible for all the actions and projects under his or her purview as a senior leader. As an accountable leader, you define what to do rather than doing it (this may even include telling others how to do it). Such a leader must rely and trust in the ability of others to accomplish the tasks at hand. If the accountable leader cannot make the shift from responsible to accountable, he or she is likely to fall short in achieving the results expected of them.[18] In my own experience as a leader, one of the primary reasons a leader cannot make the leap from responsibility to accountability is a lack of trust. You simply will not have the time to be responsible for everything. Therefore you must trust others to be responsible while you remain accountable. As we discuss the Mercy Cycle in the next section, my hope is you will come to appreciate greatly the power of trust and its place in leading with mercy. More importantly, I hope you will note and appreciate the mutually reinforcing and beneficial relationship between trust and mercy.

The Mercy Cycle

So what does this distinction between responsibility and accountability have to do with leading with mercy? We stated in the chapter on leading by example that people led with compassion are more productive, more willing to take risks and consider new solutions to problems, more trustworthy, and more trusting. People led with mercy are then arguably more responsible. If I were an executive leader charged with accountability for the results of the teams and people under my charge, would I not want colleagues with these characteristics? Letting others be responsible while you remain accountable is a risky, but necessary, endeavor. So why not set the conditions so that those to whom you are relinquishing responsibility are people who are themselves trustworthy and responsible?

The sense of responsibility that leading with mercy can em-power has significant implications for team performance. When individuals are more responsible in their work, it can be contagious. Responsible people want to work with other responsible people and are motivated to cooperate and collaborate with one another for the good of the organization and team.[19] The implications are clear – just like success breeds success, responsibility and accountability breed more of the same.

The implications for responsibility are just as great for the leader as they are for the employee and team. As a leader that is account-able for the results of others, you need confidence that your team is performing and achieving the desired results without your constant supervision. Successful executives need to free up time and energy to lead. For the executive, the definition of work is no longer rolling up your sleeves and "mowing the lawn" as Eblin writes, but rather, managing and leading the success of the landscaping business (to continue the analogy). You, the leader, have to let go of responsibility and pick up accountability.[20] In my firm we call this process working yourself out of a job. In order to progress to the next level you have to teach and develop someone (or more than one person) to take on your responsibilities so that you have the time to take on greater roles. It can be very unnerving, because you are moving out of your comfort zone by focusing on tasks other than those that made you successful to begin with, and you are making yourself vulnerable by showing that someone else can do your job in the hopes that you will move up in the organization. It is a leap of faith – and faith requires trust.

In taking on greater responsibility (or accountability) perhaps lies the greatest value and lesson in the framework of leading with mercy.

The merciful (and successful) leader is accountable, good and bad, for his organization. Passing the buck or casting stones is a significant career derailer, so much so that Marshall Goldsmith calls it a "terrifying hybrid" flaw that combines a need to be right all the time, making excuses, and punishing the messenger, among other flaws. Goldsmith argues that a leader's inability to be accountable is as negative a trait for a business leader as brainpower, courage, and resourcefulness are positive traits for the leader.[21] Moreover, it is a very visible trait to colleagues that diminishes greatly a leader's ability to earn the right to lead.

When I was a company commander in the army, my battalion commander would stop me, or my fellow company commanders mid-sentence, if we used the word "I" to take credit for an accomplishment. He admonished us to only say "I" if we are taking responsibility for a failure or shortcoming in our organization; if we are speaking of an accomplishment – be it our own or that of someone else on our team – use the word "we." At first I found it rather frustrating and semantic, but in time I came to greatly appreciate the lesson in humility and accountability.

Chade-Meng Tan of Google (Meng is a former Google engineer and now part of their talent team) notes some compelling observations and research about the link between humility and successful leadership. Meng cites Bill George, former CEO of Medtronic. George believes the transition from "I" to "we" that my battalion commander demanded of his company commanders is a necessary transformation for one to become an effective leader. George claims this shift from "I" to "we" "is the most important process leaders go through in becoming authentic." Meng adds that the practice of compassion itself is a shift from "self to others." If the organization and leader is all about "I," then the success of the organization (and the leader) is limited to his or her ability and vision.[22]

Meng also notes a study by Jim Collins, author of the book, *Good to Great: Why Some Companies Make the Leap ... and Others Don't.* Collins' team identified every Fortune 500 company from 1965 to 1995 focusing on companies that were initially "good" but became "great." Collins defines great as outperforming the general market by a factor of three or more for fifteen years or more. A common factor in these great companies was a particular set of leadership characteristics. Collins' team found the leaders of great companies have great ambition (not a big surprise, right?) ... and personal humility. In other words these leaders were driven by success but not their own success, but the success of the organization and "greater good."[23]

Figure 2. The Mercy Cycle.

Leading with mercy, it turns out, makes good business sense and has the potential to create a self-perpetuating cycle of success (Figure 2). If we know that leading with mercy fosters a workforce that is more responsible, more productive, and more trustworthy (and thus the organization will arguably have fewer shortcomings and failures), then leading with mercy makes sense for the organization, its people, and even your own professional development.

Cast No Stones

In the context of leading with mercy, responsibility and accountability are incredibly powerful. Christians believe that mercy was physically manifest in Jesus Christ. We believe God "gave His only Son, so that everyone who believes in him may not perish but might have eternal life."[24] That mercy is so powerful because even though we deserved punishment for our sins, He took on the blame and ultimate penalty. The Buddha is said to have felt so much compassion for the sick and suffering that he gave up his life of royalty for an austere life, seeking enlightenment in the hopes it would eliminate human suffering and frailties.[25] Whether you believe in these figures as spiritual or religious leaders is not the point. Even as historical figures, they are impressive examples of leading with mercy. I am not so bold as to claim that leading with mercy in the world of business is on par with the passion of Christ or the sacrifices of other significant world figures. I am claiming that the merciful and responsible leader gets credit for the successes of his team and should likewise be accountable for and accept consequences of his people's failures, whether intentional or not, whether avoidable or not, whether predicted or not (nothing saps morale like an "I told you so.").

Lest I leave you thinking that mercy is only for the spiritual, consider the following:

Be hard on yourself, but lenient on others. Mercy inspires loyalty. Deepen your capacity as a leader by observing the Secret of Restraint: Be first to forgive.

Leaders who reprimand their followers for trifling transgressions hurt only themselves. But leaders who seek to grow in spirit as much as in influence observe the Secret of Kindness: Forgive small failures.

Guess who said this. A monk? A self-help guru? A pastor? No. These are the words of a 16th-century samurai, Toyotomi Hideyoshi. Hideyoshi was born to a farming family in 1536. He was an unlikely samurai, small of stature even for that time, and not physically gifted. By 1590 he was the supreme ruler of what is today Japan. His success is not credited to mastery of military strategy or martial arts, but rather to his "remarkable talent for organizational leadership [and] genius at attracting, hiring, managing, compensating, and promoting" within his army.[26]

Being a merciful or compassionate leader does not mean you should never reprimand or even fire an employee. If an individual is not able to maintain standards, especially legal and ethical ones, and contribute positively to the team and the business, then the best decision may very well be to part ways. Where leading with mercy fits into this equation is making the effort to help a struggling employee be successful. Are we clearly communicating our standards and expectations? Have we given the employee time and resources to meet and exceed our goals and expectations? Do we know the employee well enough to understand whether the issue is one of competence or attitude? Do we know if there is a personal challenge in that individual's life that makes performing to their potential a challenge? If at the end of the proverbial day, we have led with mercy and given an individual every reasonable opportunity to succeed – and it simply is not working, for whatever reason – then again, terminating or reassigning that person may be the right decision. It is not an either/or – you can lead your organization with mercy and still maintain and demand excellence in your organization.

I'm Sorry

I can think of no more appropriate way to end a chapter on responsibility within the framework of leading with mercy than with a section on apologizing. Just like a sincere "I'm sorry, will you forgive me?" is incredibly powerful in a personal relationship, it is also a powerful leadership tool.

Marshall Goldsmith, a prominent executive coach, regards apologizing as "the most magical, healing, restorative gesture human beings can make." He goes on to say it is the foundation of his work in coaching executives to be even more successful. Pretty powerful stuff, with a direct correlation to business.[27]

In the previous section I offered that a leader gets credit for his team's success and should therefore take responsibility for his team's failures. Like all of us, leaders make mistakes. It does not have to be as egregious as avoiding responsibility. It could be forgetting to follow up on a promised action or a voicemail. It could be chronic tardiness to meetings. I have witnessed no more humble and impactful an act than a leader who offers his colleagues an apology for his mistakes. Critics might counter that apologizing makes the leader appear weak or not confident in his actions. I offer that it makes the leader more respected and makes team members feel valued (to my earlier point, business is personal). Psychologists agree that an apology benefits both the giver and the receiver. An article in *Psychology Today* offers an easy way to offer a sincere apology:

❖ Regret: A statement of regret for having caused the hurt or damage (I would add for being disrespectful in the case of wasting someone's time or ignoring them).

❖ Responsibility: An acceptance of responsibility for actions.

❖ Remedy: A statement of willingness to remedy the situation. [28]

Questions to consider about being a responsible and accountable leader.

1. Who bears responsibility when there is a failure or shortcoming in my organization?

2. How can I better develop others so they can grow professionally?

3. How do my actions convey trust to those I lead?

4. How often do I say "we" vs. "I?"

5. When is the last time I said, "I'm sorry?"

CHAPTER FOUR

CLARITY OF VISION

Wisdom is nothing more than the marriage
of intelligence and compassion.
– Vera Nazarian

In a *The New York Times* online editorial, Tony Schwartz wrote this:

There are some deep and complicated reasons that only a small percentage of employees around the world feel truly engaged and satisfied at work. There are also some simple solutions that leaders and managers can introduce at virtually no cost that would make any workplace more humane and desirable – and, in all likelihood, also increase profitability.

Schwartz goes on to list several solutions such as: respect and value your employees, measure value not hours, and help people "build more renewal into their lives" (we will address that more in

Chapter 5).[29] I would like to add another: provide your people clarity of vision.

Anyone who has ever tried to draft, socialize, finalize, and articulate a vision statement knows this is easier said than done. Some of us get cold chills at the mere mention of the word. But what is a book about leadership and business without a discussion of vision? To take it a step further, a discussion about vision – and clarity of vision – is also essential to a book about leading with mercy.

Andrew Neitlich, President of the Center for Executive Coaching, says that vision provides a leader with "focus and direction over time" and that a clear, compelling vision inspires "employees to go the extra mile." He goes on to offer several questions a leader and his team should answer in crafting a vision. What problems are we solving in your market? What does our organization do better than any other? What value do we bring to our customers? How much market share can we claim? What key milestones must we achieve along the path of achieving our vision?[30]

Kouzes and Posner discuss in depth the importance of finding a common purpose, listening to others in crafting a vision, and making the vision "a cause for commitment." Research shows that for many, work is not just about earning money, but rather, people have a desire for positive impact. I offer that the way to meet that desire is to provide your people clarity of vision. [31]

In a study published in 2011, Dr. Katherine Hyatt, an Assistant Professor of Business at Reinhardt University, reports there is "a significant positive relationship … between inspiring a shared vision and perceived organization support. She goes on to conclude that the importance of practices like sharing vision "cannot be underscored."[32]

So we have arguably established the need for vision, more importantly the need for a compelling vision. You did not need to buy a book about leading with mercy to learn that. So how do leading with mercy and clarity of vision tie together? We established with the Mercy Cycle that leading with mercy can create a workforce and leadership team that are more responsible, which then builds trust; an organization of people grounded in responsibility and trust very likely has higher morale, which leads to greater productivity. Finally, people that are led with mercy are more apt to take the risks necessary to discover new ideas and solutions, thus leading the organization to greater success. Retired Army General Stan McChrystal recounts a story that illustrates well the power of trust and its impact on an individual. McChrystal tells the story of a time he had to brief a superior on "a plan for relief of a threatened U.S. position in Latin America." As McChrystal prepared to brief his superior, the boss simply asked him if it was a good plan. McChrystal indicated it was a good plan, to which the boss responded, "[then] I don't need a brief; I trust you." McChrystal recalled the moment as "more powerful than anything else he could have said or done."[33]

Vision, we said earlier – especially a clear, compelling vision – is about inspiring individuals and organizations to achievement, contributions, and impact beyond that which perhaps they can even imagine. Ponder this for a minute: Leading with mercy can ultimately lead to greater success through risk-taking in an organization; a clear vision inspires people to achieve the previously unimagined.

In the military there is a doctrinal term called *force multiplier*. The official definition is:

> *A capability that, when added to and employed by a combat force, significantly increases the combat potential of that force and thus enhances the probability of successful mission accomplishment.*[34]

In other words, the sum is greater than the parts – a capability that when added to another compounds its impact. For example, an armor battalion (a unit of tanks) is a powerful force with great firepower – but tanks need room to navigate, and "tankers" (soldiers that operate tanks) are not trained to dismount and seize terrain (actually secure a piece of land). An infantry battalion is trained for that very mission, but even inside its vehicles (which are less armored than tanks) it is more vulnerable to enemy firepower than an armor unit. Both armor and infantry are vulnerable to enemy artillery or air power. However, an air force fighter squadron can attack enemy positions from a significant range before the armor and infantry units are even in range of enemy fire. So in this scenario, infantry and air power are force multipliers for the armor battalion – because combined their combat potential is greater than that of just the armor unit.

Now let us modify the official military definition of force multiplier to serve our purpose:

> *Clarity of vision, when added to leading with mercy practiced by a leader, significantly increases the potential of an organization and thus enhances the probability that the organization will be successful.*

In other words, within the framework of leading with mercy, clarity of vision greatly increases the chances that individuals and organizations will achieve success.

I will end this chapter with a case study in clarity of vision within the framework of leading with mercy. The organization in this case study is characterized as breaking "every rule in Business 101 except attention to quality." Of course, every leader worth a lick knows you have to focus on quality – that is Business 101, is it not? It is, but as successful CEO and author August Turak writes, quality is not just about the output or product of your business. In this case, the emphasis on quality and the resulting success come from a rebalancing of a qualitative vs. quantitative approach to the entire business, not just the output. Turak is clear to say that the quantitative approach is important, but many of today's executives have created an imbalance to the great neglect of the qualitative approach. The qualitative approach is about being faithful to your people, your customers, and your product. In today's terms, Turak argues, it is being authentic.[35]

The business in this case study is the abbey of St. Sixtus of Westvleteren in Belgium. Yes, monks. What is their business? Well, ultimately their business (they would call it their life) is God ... but what they make and sell a lot of is ... beer. Yes, I have managed to incorporate beer into a book about leadership and business. The monks of St. Sixtus have brewed beer since 1836 and one brand is consistently rated as one of the top five beers in the world. The revenue they generate from sales of the beer covers the cost of running and maintaining the abbey, and the rest is generally given to the poor. They could very easily charge and get more for their product. Their most expensive brand goes for about $2.75 per bottle. It is sold (illegally, since the monks ask that their beer not be resold) in bars for $8-$12 per bottle. That is a markup any businessperson would smile about.[36]

Monks are not the only ones that believe a focus on "service and selflessness" and a long-term view (vs. something like quarterly earnings statements) is good business. To wit, none other than Warren Buffett annually focuses his shareholders on the long-term vision of Berkshire Hathaway. One of the benefits of this long-term view (vision) for Buffett is a reputation for being highly ethical and trustworthy. So much so that he gets a "Buffett Discount" when he acquires companies. Sellers have sold to Buffett, despite better offers, because they trust Buffett will be considerate of their companies and "treat them honorably."[37]

In sum, clarity of vision and leading with mercy complement one another as impactful business practices. Leading with mercy starts the Mercy Cycle (described in Chapter Three) that leads to more responsible, trustworthy, productive, and successful teams and organizations. Providing such a group of people clarity of vision gives them a purpose to which to aspire. Striving toward such a purpose (achieving the vision) leads an organization to greatness. Greatness benefits each individual and the organization.

Questions to consider about providing clear vision.

1. What are my aspirations for my organization?

2. To what do those I lead aspire?

3. What would an employee say if I asked them to describe our vision?

4. How have I prepared my organization and my people for success?

5. What would happen if I focused more on the long-term results?

CHAPTER FIVE

LEAD FROM THE HEART

Love and compassion are necessities, not luxuries.
Without them, humanity cannot survive.
–Dalai Lama

"Leadership is not an affair of the head. Leadership is an affair of the heart."[38] If you have continued reading to this chapter, 1) thank you very much, and 2) you are likely not surprised at the quote above. You may be surprised at the source. Given some of my other sources, you may be expecting a religious or spiritual source. In fact, this quote ends a book by Kouzes and Posner. Their book *The Leadership Challenge: How to Make Extraordinary Things Happen in Organizations* is in its fifth edition, having sold over 2 million copies in over 20 languages in the past 25 years. The authors are both renowned business professors (Kouzes a current dean, Posner a former dean) and leadership experts at Leavey School of Business, Santa Clara University. I tout their titles and accomplishments to reinforce that my notion of leading with mercy is not just a personal quest or spiritual journey; rather, the elements of leading with mercy (what I have called a framework) are well-researched and documented by experts far more studied and intelligent than I am. When I read the term "affair of the heart" I thought to myself, "Are they saying this is about love?" Yes, Kouzes and Posner claim that leadership is about love:

> *And what sustains the leader? From what source comes the leader's courage? The answer is love. Leaders are in love – in love with the people who do the work, with what their organizations produce, and with their customers.*[39]

But do people come to work to be loved? Do they expect to be loved? Should leaders love the people they work with? Yes, and the love that leaders have for the people they are privileged to lead is a selfless, merciful love. Early Christians used a Greek word for love, *agape* (in theological circles it is often called agape love) to distinguish from other types of love (e.g. romantic love). Agape is a "selfless, sacrificial, unconditional love."[40] This type of love is also similar to what you might expect from Robert Greenleaf's "servant-leader" – or the leader who wants to serve first and then aspires to lead.[41] It is this type of love that the merciful leader feels for those he leads. It is this type of love that people being led desire from the person leading them.

Tony Schwartz and Christine Porath wrote an article for the *New York Times' Sunday Review*, entitled "Why You Hate Your Job." In a follow-up article, Schwartz writes how he was "stunned" at how poorly people feel they are treated at work based on the nearly 500 "overwhelmingly acid" comments he received after the initial article. Schwartz offered some suggestions, based on his experience as a business owner and studying and working with large organizations, to make the workplace a better place to work. Several of his suggestions are what I call leading from the heart. Here are some excerpts:

- ❖ "Respect and hold the value of every person who works for you … feeling cared for and encouraged to grow builds trust and loyalty."

- ❖ "Help people build more renewal in their lives, on and off the job."

- ❖ "Seek to define all jobs in ways that feel meaningful and significant … recognizing the desire we all have to contribute to something larger than ourselves."[42]

Schwartz's recommendations are about leading with mercy.

Eric Shinseki, retired army general and former Secretary of the Veterans Administration, also talks about love in the context of leadership. Shinseki fought and led soldiers in combat. In his retirement speech after 37 years in the U.S. Army, Shinseki said the following:

You must love those you lead before you can be an effective leader. You can certainly command without that sense of commitment, but you cannot lead without it; and without leadership, command is a hollow experience - a vacuum often filled with mistrust and arrogance.[43]

General Shinseki is talking about leading from the heart. (A colleague of mine who worked directly for Shinseki – and who made me aware of Shinseki's retirement speech – agreed wholeheartedly).[44]

Most of us would probably agree that leading from the heart sounds like a decent enough idea – who does not like to be the nice person saying nice things about others and making them feel good about themselves? For soldiers that train and fight in dangerous conditions, we can easily understand that those circumstances would create strong emotional bonds. But that is no way to run a business, is it? For those of use that need a more compelling case than "it feels good," consider this: successful organizations generally attract and retain talented people. My own experience is that talented people, even in modest economic times, generally have a choice about where they work. Recruiting, on-boarding, and training new people cost your business money, and if retention in your business is a problem, it is a cost you are not recovering. In short, there are compelling business reasons for leading from the heart (a word of caution: if you are leading from the heart because it is good business, be sincere about it … otherwise do not bother). I will address the business case for leading from the heart in more detail in the final chapter.

So assuming that people want to feel respected and valued at work, if not even loved, what are some tangible ways that we can lead from the heart? The list is a long one but I will highlight three:

❖ Recognize, encourage, and celebrate

❖ Give back

❖ Tough love

I have been on the receiving and giving (at least I have striven to be) end of leadership from the heart. Honestly, I am not sure which perspective is more rewarding. What I am sure of is that there are simple, personal, powerful, and compassionate ways to interact with people. I am also sure that if these acts are at first just a business practice (but heed my earlier warning about sincerity), once you reap the joy of giving and receiving from the heart, these practices for respecting and valuing your colleagues will positively impact your life and theirs (and your business). They will be part of who you are as a person and a leader.

Recognize, Encourage, and Celebrate

In the summer of 1992 I was a rising senior Army ROTC cadet attending Advanced Camp (now called the Leadership Development and Assessment Course) at Fort Bragg, North Carolina. It is a culminating training and assessment course that lasts about five weeks. A cadet's performance at this course has a significant impact on his or her future status (regular army, active, or reserve) and specialty in the army. I was particularly anxious because I had missed a semester of training because I was, at the time, medically disqualified to receive a commission in the army. I was concerned that I had fallen behind my peers in the necessary tactics. My anxiety was magnified when I received a negative spot report (a report from an evaluator that you were deficient in an area) early in the five-week course. An evaluator claimed I had committed an unsafe act during a rappelling exercise (to this day I believe it was the other way around ... but had it not played out the way it did, I would not have this story to tell). I was devastated.

A week or so later, as part of a confidence course, we were required to climb a tower, crawl out on a rope suspended 40 feet over

✦ 40 ✦

a small lake, tap a sign with the word "Ranger" painted on it, hang from the rope with our feet dangling, and then drop into the lake. A fair enough task to ask of a future leader of soldiers, no? Fair indeed -- but I cannot swim, and I am afraid of water.

As a safety precaution, prior to crawling onto the rope, we were required to call out, "strong swimmer," "weak swimmer," or "non-swimmer." In my most bellowing command voice I exclaimed, "non-swimmer." During the demonstration of this particular event, a non-swimmer was greeted by divers once he dropped into the water (for the record, that did not happen). I climbed onto the rope, pulled myself toward the Ranger sign, tapped the sign, swung my legs off the rope, and fell (I swung a little too much) into the lake 40 feet below. I was wearing a life jacket and after paddling furiously (because, again, no divers greeted me) to the edge of the lake, I spit out all the water in my mouth and thanked the good Lord for dry land. As I regained my composure my tactical sergeant (and active duty non-commissioned officer assigned to our company) approached me. He took me to the side and handed me a slip of paper. Another spot report. This time, however, it was a positive spot report in which the sergeant recognized my courage for negotiating the obstacle as a non-swimmer.

I tell this story not as a tale of courage (far from it, to be honest) but as a story of the power of recognition. I was demoralized from the previous incident and convinced that I had blown any opportunity at a regular army commission in the branch of my choice. In a matter of minutes with one little piece of paper, the sergeant restored my confidence and I went on to complete the course with the highest rating.

Just about everyone needs and likes to recognized for their work, contributions, and successes. Part of knowing your people is knowing how they like to be acknowledged. By how, I do not just mean what material recognition (e.g., hand-written note, monetary, time off, a verbal "thank you," etc.) but also the manner in which it is delivered (e.g. large or small gathering, privately, surprise event, etc.). Knowing this can help guide you in deciding with what and how to recognize them. Before I provide some examples, a brief note on formal awards and recognition programs. In their book on engagement strategies, Beverly Kaye and Sharon Jordan-Evans, warn "if an employee expects it, it may no longer be viewed as a reward."[45] This does not mean every awards presentation should be a surprise, but rather if the recognition has become pro forma (e.g. an annual holiday bonus or a perk offered to everyone with certain tenure or position) then people are unlikely to view it as recognition of a particular success or contribution. That said, here are some examples of recognition I have found to be very personal and powerful based on my reaction receiving them, and more importantly, feedback from people whom I have recognized.

❖ Hand-written thank you note, particularly one that is sent to a home address (and addressed by your hand). By far, this is the act of recognition that seems to be the most powerful. For me it was the thought that someone with a very hectic schedule took the time to write me a personal note. I have a particularly thoughtful one pinned to my desk. In an era of e-mail, chat, texts, and posts a personal note is often particularly appreciated.

❖ Gift card to a store or restaurant you know the individual enjoys. Again, it is the personal touch and recognition by the receiver that you know something about them and who they are.

❖ Paid time off. Who does not enjoy an extra day or two of time away from the office? For our most prestigious individual award, my company gives several days of additional vacation time, airfare, and spending money for a trip to places like the Caribbean or Hawaii. Not all businesses can afford this, but the point is that it is special recognition for a significant contribution.

I could list several more, but you are likely more creative than I am, so have some fun with it. Based on what you know about an employee – what would they really appreciate?

Similar to recognition, another wonderful way to lead from the heart is to celebrate the joys of your people's lives and acknowledge the sadness. Again, this is about knowing the person. If someone is particularly sensitive about birthdays, then maybe a public rendition of "Happy Birthday" is not a great idea. Particularly in acknowledging sad or tragic events, we obviously want to be sensitive to our employees' privacy and emotional states. I would offer, however, that you not let that be an excuse to do nothing. For consideration, I offer a few ways I have seen leaders celebrate joys and milestones, and acknowledge the less-joyful times in people's lives. You will notice they may not be that different from how you would treat a friend or family member in a similar situation.

❖ Take someone to a nice lunch or dinner to celebrate a birthday or an anniversary with your company.

❖ Have baby or bridal (or groom) showers.

❖ Send flowers, or a sweet treat, or fruit, or a nice gift upon the birth of a child ... or any other reason!

❖ If you are invited to a wedding or a funeral, attend or at least acknowledge such a significant event.

❖ Make a contribution to a cause if an employee has asked a loved one to be remembered in such a way.

I know many of you are thinking this is really obvious stuff. Unfortunately, for some it is not. For others we get mired in the daily grind and forget to make time for these personal acts of compassion. If you do not have the time, make it ... please.

We have recognized and celebrated. A third thoughtful way to lead from the heart is to encourage. Encourage your people to use the vacation time they have earned. Do not make them feel guilt about it – we all need time to unwind and decompress. Encourage moms and dads to attend a kindergarten graduation or volunteer for playground duty every once in a while (trust me, they will not want to do it more than every once in a while). If your type of work allows it, provide your colleagues some flexibility in their schedules and encourage them to build an exercise routine into their week. Finally, encourage them to give back. Whether it is volunteering for a cause like a homeless shelter, kitchen, or an animal rescue, or giving time to their kids by volunteering at a school event or coaching a youth sports team. Even better, get together a group from work and volunteer together. Encourage a spirit of compassion and service. You, your people, your business, your customers, and stakeholders, and your communities will be better of for it. I dedicate a separate section to it below.

Give Back

Ut Prosim – That I May Serve. This is the motto of Virginia Tech, from where I graduated. As a member of the Virginia Tech Corps of Cadets, this motto took on a significant meaning for me as I trained to serve my country in the U.S. Army. The spirit of service is found throughout the university (and undoubtedly many others) through the Corps of Cadets, service groups, sororities and fraternities, and other student organizations. I was not astute enough to notice it at the time, but as I reflect back on my time at Virginia Tech, the students that served others seemed more confident, more fulfilled, more engaged, and academically more successful.

Corporate Social Responsibility (CSR) is a popular buzzword in the business world, as well it should be. There are several tangible business benefits to practicing CSR, be it sustainability, corporate giving, or volunteerism. The benefits include favorable branding and reputation, in some cases tax benefits, and increased employee engagement. A 2011 study by Deloitte confirmed many of these benefits including the links between corporate-sponsored or advocated volunteerism and increased "corporate culture." People that feel positive about the corporate culture claim to be more loyal to the organization, more satisfied in their career, and likely to recommend their organization to a friend. [46] Indeed these are positive, measurable results that any business leader and human resources professional would welcome in their business.

There are also less tangible, and more powerful, benefits to service, volunteering, and giving back. There is something in the human spirit that drives us to giving – for many of us it just feels right or good. We know that mercy and compassion are good, and right, and just. It warms our hearts. And the needs and causes are obviously many.

Pro bono work is another way for businesses to give back. I am very proud of a program my employer hosts as part of our leadership development program. As part of an executive development program, teams of mid-level executives are assigned a pro bono consulting engagement. The benefit to our firm is great consulting and leadership experience. The recipients receive the benefit of free consulting from a group of very talented and diverse executives. One of my direct reports completed this program. His team was assigned to assist a non-profit organization named, *Give an Hour* (giveanhour. org). *Give an Hour* itself is a powerful example of giving back. Their mission is to "provide free mental health services to U.S. military personnel and families."[47] The way *Give an Hour* provides these services is through a network of nationwide mental health professionals who volunteer their time and expertise. I had the pleasure of meeting the founder and president of *Give an Hour,* Dr. Barbara Van Dahlen – she is understandably proud that *Give an Hour* providers have volunteered over 140,000 hours of service (valued at over $14M) to service members and veterans who come home with invisible wounds of war, and to the families that love them.

In my own experiences volunteering with my team, I have found I see a very genuine, relaxed, and happy side of my colleagues that I may not always encounter in the work environment. Some may argue that creating such a personal bond or letting down your guard weakens your authority to lead and makes you second-guess difficult decisions. I offer that such experiences build strong bonds of respect and loyalty (both ways). As for difficult decisions ... that's part of being a leader. A decision should not be less difficult because you do not have a bond with the people it affects. Whether you know them or not, you should consider the implications on them.

The benefits of giving back are clear – giving back benefits businesses, our people, and the community and organizations that are served. So why not lead from the heart and encourage giving back in your organization?

Tough Love

By now some of you are ready to give me a hug because you are convinced I am a corporate teddy bear. This guy was a soldier? This guy is an executive? To make it even worse, I have studied martial arts and coached numerous youth sports, to include some bruisers like football and lacrosse. So this is where I try to redeem my man-card and rub some dirt on it, as they say (I am in no way implying that only men can give out tough love, quite the contrary, but I am not sure person-card means anything to anyone). Often when discussing merciful or compassionate leadership the conversation turns to taking care of our people. This is certainly a worthy topic, but is one we as leaders must navigate thoughtfully. In my early experiences as a young leader and as someone who has mentored and coached other leaders, I found that one of the common mistakes we make is believing that "taking care of my people" means shielding them from tough love and simply giving them what they want. Sometimes it is an innocent and well-intended practice of an inexperienced leader. Other times it is an excuse, even for a more experienced leader, to avoid conflict and difficult conversations (for me, it was a little bit of both).

For many years I have practiced and studied (unfortunately more study than practice recently) the Japanese martial art, Aikido. Aikido is primarily an art of self-defense where the practitioner rarely initiates an attack. Rather, in Aikido you defend yourself by redirecting your opponent's energy or otherwise using it against him or her, resulting in hip throws, joint locks or manipulation, and other interesting techniques. The attack ideally ends with the attacker in a precarious situation such as a joint lock where the defender could easily inflict more pain or even permanent damage. This, however, is where Aikido differs from other martial arts. In the case of Aikido, the defender applies only enough force and pain to control and hopefully de-escalate the situation. Students of Aikido feel a great responsibility to not hurt their attacker (or partner, in a training situation) any more than necessary. I offer my experience with Aikido as an example analogous to practicing tough love within the framework of leading with mercy. As we lead with mercy there will be times where we have to inflict some figurative pain. In the world of leadership, this "pain" comes in the form of communicating and maintaining standards, correcting and disciplining poor behavior or practices, but always allowing for room to experience and learn from mistakes. Just as the Aikidoist feels responsible for the well-being of the attacker, we as the leader are responsible for the well-being and development of our people, even when inflicting some tough love.

Many of us have our definition of tough love. In the framework of leading with mercy, my definition is about setting high standards, communicating clearly those standards, exemplifying them, teaching and empowering others in those standards, and maintaining accountability for achieving them. All of these objectives require tough love at one time or another. To be clear, tough love is not an excuse to be rude, disrespectful, sarcastic, or otherwise unprofessional and unmerciful in communicating and enforcing standards. Tough love, in the framework of leading with mercy, is giving our people the support, resources, and tools to give them reasonable opportunity to meet standards or improve performance if it is substandard. Tough love does not mean you will never counsel, officially reprimand, or terminate an employee. If after reasonable and sincere efforts the employee is not able to meet standards, then terminating their employment may well be the proper decision. Obviously, not making the decision to terminate a chronically underperforming employee is bad for the business; but perhaps more importantly it will negatively impact morale of colleagues who are performing to (or hopefully beyond) your standards.

Tough yet compassionate love is not just about rehabilitating underperforming team members. Tough love is about expecting the best from yourself and your people, and giving them the tools and resources to continually learn and grow in their profession. It is about challenging and stretching your people to perform better and grow more than they think possible. There is a powerful scene in the 2006 movie *Facing the Giants*. The movie is in general a great example of leading with mercy, and one particular scene illustrates tough love in the context of a high football team practice. In the scene the head football coach is frustrated with a talented young man who is an informal leader of the team. The young man is not confident in his abilities and his lack of confidence manifests as an "I can't do it" attitude that affects his teammates because of his influence as an informal leader. In a practice drill, the coach blindfolds the young man and tells him to bear-crawl a relatively short distance with a teammate on his back. The young man quickly complains of being tired and unable to go any further. The coach encourages him to keep going just a bit further, then just a bit further than that. When the young man eventually collapses from sheer exhaustion and fatigue he is upset that he has disappointed his coach and teammates. At that point the head coach tells the young man to take off his blindfold. The young football player has crawled the entire length of the field with a 160-pound teammate on his back.

The lessons in this example are several. One, while the coach raised his voice, he never used disrespectful or derogatory language; he genuinely felt this player had more to give and was sincere in wanting the player to succeed. Two, the player learned that he was capable of much more than he had ever thought possible. And third, the player's teammates witnessed an example of tough love that motivated a teammate, and a role model on the team, to accomplish a significant feat; which in turn motivated them to try harder and accomplish greater things themselves. All of these lessons are easily translated into benefits of tough love in a business environment.

Those of you with any experiences on a team (business, military, volunteer, sports, etc.) have likely heard someone say: "That person has a lot of potential …." That statement is sometimes followed with an "and" but often with a "but" or "if only." By leading with mercy and tough love, we can address this statement in a productive manner that develops the person and benefits the organization. In some cases the potential means they seem to get "it" but need us to teach the fundamentals. A sports analogy would be a gifted athlete who has never played football. The athlete may be strong, fast, and nimble, but may not know how to read a block or run a route. In this case it benefits us as leaders to spend some time teaching this person the basics (blocking and tackling, to continue the analogy) of the business we are in. Perhaps this person would benefit from a mentor or from shadowing a more experienced employee.

In the scenario above, our love does not really need to be that tough because the individual really has no reason to push back. Let us explore a scenario that may require much tougher love. In other cases potential may mean that someone has succeeded at one level, but for one reason or another, is not succeeding at the next level. Marshall Goldsmith wrote an entire book for leaders who want to "take it to the next level." The title of his book – *What Got You Here Won't Get You There* – reveals the secret of engaging with an employee who has not quite been able to break through to the next level.

The reason this scenario might take tougher love is that, as Goldsmith points out, these types of people have often already been successful, so they are confident in their abilities and convinced that what got them here (skills, behaviors, attitudes, etc.) will get them there. Marshall identifies 20 habits that may hold back these types of people. Many of these 20 habits – such as passing judgment, refusing to express regret, and failure to express gratitude – are the antithesis of leading with mercy. So in such a case it may take some time, effort, and tough love to convince them otherwise. Such tough love might include development goals aimed at modifying these behaviors (or stated more accurately, adopting new behaviors to replace the less desirable ones).[48]

Questions to consider about leading from the heart.

1. When is the last time I thanked or congratulated someone on my team?

2. How well do I know the people that work for me?

3. How have I encouraged my people to give back?

4. How have I ensured my team members know what is expected of them?

5. What can I do to help a struggling team member be successful; or a high-performing colleague to be even more successful?

CHAPTER SIX

LEAD FROM THE HEAD: THE BUSINESS CASE FOR LEADING WITH MERCY

*A little bit of mercy makes the world
less cold and more just.*
– Pope Francis

In the introduction I stated it is my hope that this book will convince you of the business case and impact of leading with mercy. For some of you, leading with mercy has (I hope "had" instead of "has" by this point) no place in leadership and business. For others, the case for mercy and compassion in organizational leadership "felt right" but you were not convinced it was good business. If I have not yet convinced you of its power, both personal and professional, I will give it one more try with a discussion of the business case and positive impact of leading with mercy, with an emphasis on quantitative results and metrics. In doing so I will cite experts and sources in the field of leadership, business, and related areas so as not to offer a case of "because I said so." That does not work with my children, and I know it will not work here either.

So for those if us that tend to lead from the head, what is the business case for leading with mercy? Consider the following recent headlines or article titles and excerpts:

❖ "Trust and Bottom Line: How Does Paying Attention to The Human Element in Business Improve Your Bottom Line?" (2009):

> *Measuring the exact costs of the lack of trust* [See Chapter Two for the impact of trust in the Lead With Mercy framework and the Mercy Cycle] *can be difficult because the ramifications are so wide and long lasting. But, we can make conservative estimates of the costs in dollars and time and discover that the potential return of increased trust is well worth the effort.* <u>*Even a 10% decrease in meeting time resulting from improved group trust will make a substantial financial and productivity difference in a small department over the course of a year. Such a decrease is equivalent to adding several hours of available work time per week for an entire team*</u> *(emphasis added).*[49]

❖ "Managing Compassionately" (2012):

> *Of all the management principles I have adopted over the years, either through direct experience or learning from others, there is one I aspire to live by more than any other. I say "aspire" because as much as I'd like to do it consistently and without fail, given the natural ebb and flow of day-to-day operations and challenges, and the subsequent range of responses that follow, I find this particular*

*principle harder to practice consistently than others. <u>That princi-
ple is managing compassionately</u> (emphasis added).* [50]

❖ "The Rise of Compassionate Management (Finally)" (2013):

<u>*The evidence also shows that compassion boosts employee well-be-
ing and health*</u> — *another important contributor to the bottom
line [emphasis added]. And as my good friend Dr. Edward Hal-
lowell shows in his book* Connect: 12 Vital Ties that Open Your
Heart, Lengthen Your Life and Deepen Your Soul, *the more we
compassionately connect, the better we feel, and the more others
are there to support us when we need it, as even the most seemingly
invulnerable of us someday, inevitably, will.*[51]

❖ "Companies that Practice 'Conscious Capitalism' Perform
10x Better" (2013):

The 18 publicly traded [conscious] companies out of the 28
<u>outperformed the S&P 500 index by a factor of 10.5</u> (em-
phasis added) over the years 1996-2011. And why, in the
end, should that be a surprise? Conscious companies treat
their stakeholders better. As a consequence, their suppliers
are happier to do business with them. Employees are more
engaged, productive, and likely to stay. These companies are
more welcome in their communities and their customers are
more satisfied and loyal. The most conscious companies give
more, and they get more in return. <u>The inescapable conclu-
sion: it pays to care, widely and deeply</u> (emphasis added).[52]

❖ "Why We Need Kind and Compassionate Leaders" (2012):

*Compassion is not only a very enjoyable state, it is also very
pragmatic. Leaders who are more compassionate enjoy the*

benefits of building high levels of trust and influence with their people. When people know that we truly care about them, they are much more likely to follow us. <u>People that are well cared for are also more productive and more innovative. This, of course, is very helpful for the bottom line</u> [emphasis added].[53]

❖ "Cockroaches, Compassion, and Better Business Results" (2013):

A startling 37% of American workers—roughly 54 million people—have been bullied at work according to a 2007 survey by the Workplace Bullying Institute … According to a 2007 survey by Zogby International, almost 50% of the U.S. workers report they have experienced or witnessed some kind of bullying—verbal abuse, insults, threats, screaming, sarcasm or ostracism … Other studies estimate <u>the financial costs of bullying at more than $200 billion per year</u> [emphasis added].[54]

It is also important to note who is writing and publishing many of these articles. The authors include LinkedIn CEO, Jeff Weiner. The publications and blogs include *Harvard Business Review* and *Psychology Today* (while not a business source, please note the author references quantitative studies). Earlier I cited the former CEO of PUMA, Jochen Zeitz. The point being that while I do not believe we have yet turned the corner (and I would like to see just as much use of the word mercy as compassion – but beggars cannot be choosers), I argue the prevailing wind is shifting. As a business leader it is often pays positive dividends to be an early adopter as opposed to playing catch up with the competition after they have reaped the benefits. Especially in this more austere time of doing more with less, reduced budgets, and workplace efficiency, the case for leading with mercy is clear and compelling.

Higher Purpose (and Happiness)

Experts in a variety of fields – from leadership to psychology to motivation to spirituality – talk about the need for finding a higher purpose or something greater than self. We talked in Chapter Three about the shift from "I" to "we." Others, like me, talk about bringing your whole self to work (not compromising your values in the workplace) or waking up wanting to go to work (being happy about the work you do). Just like we made the argument that practicing mercy and compassion is, in great part, that transition from "I" to "we," being happy at work is about finding a higher purpose (again, a purpose other than self). In fact, Tony Hsieh, the CEO of Zappos, believes "higher purpose" is the ultimate type of happiness (and a compelling business brand). So what does all this have to do with a business case for leading with mercy? How about growing from a start-up company to a company with a billion dollars in annual revenue?[55]

That is exactly what Zappos did. Between 1999, when Zappos was founded, to 2008 its revenue grew from essentially nothing to over one billion dollars.[56] CEO Tony Hsieh is a significant proponent of the power of culture upon the success of Zappos or any business. It is also interesting to note the evolution in Zappos' brand over a decade as it grew:[57]

❖ In 1999, the Zappos brand promise was, "Largest Selection of Shoes."

❖ 2003: Customer Service

❖ 2005: Culture and Core Values as Our Platform

❖ 2007: Personal Emotional Connection

❖ 2009: Delivering Happiness

Call these brand promises soft and squishy, if you like, but the company's growth speaks for itself. Perhaps the evolution of Zappos brand is coincidental to its growth ... but perhaps it is not.

I offer that Hsieh is an example of leading with mercy, given his focus on aspiring and evolving to something greater than one's self. Hsieh describes three types of happiness: pleasure, passion, and higher purpose meaning. Pleasure, he argues, is fleeting and he describes it as "chasing the next high." Passion is the next type of happiness, and in the hierarchy of the three types is more lasting or permanent than just pleasure. Hsieh describes passion as where "peak performance meets peak engagement" or an athlete who is "in the zone." Finally, he describes higher purpose meaning as the third type of happiness, and the type of happiness that is longest lasting and most sustainable. He defines this third type of happiness as "being part of something bigger than yourself." Like other observers, Hsieh notes that people seem to spend their lives focusing on pleasure and trying to sustain it and assuming it will lead to greater happiness. Hsieh's premise is that only by pursuing higher purpose meaning can you find a sustainable happiness. If I reflect on my Christian faith, I recall this verse in the Bible: "No one has greater love than this, to lay down one's life for one's friends." Granted, this is the ultimate example of something greater than oneself; my point is that the notion of humility, sacrifice for the greater good, and ultimate happiness are not new ideas ... perhaps they are new in business and heretofore confined to the realm of the spiritual ... but there is mounting evidence that leading with mercy has a place in the realm of business and leadership also.

Go Forth and Lead with Mercy

If you made it to the end of this book, you know faith is a central part of my life. My journey of faith was a big influence in writing this book. As a Christian, it is only through God's mercy that I have been redeemed and can receive salvation. While I and other leaders cannot provide that ultimate gift of mercy, we can and should lead our organizations and our people with mercy. For those who already lead their organizations with mercy, thank you for leading by example. For those who thought it was the right thing to do but could not quite rationalize the business case in your mind, here is your excuse – go for it, starting today. For those who thought this idea was just another "interesting" idea (I say "thought" since I assume if you still think so, you never even read this chapter), give it a shot – you have little if anything to lose and a lot, literally and figuratively, to gain. Go earn the right to lead. Be accountable and give responsibility to your people. Provide your colleagues a clear vision of compassion, innovation, and success. Finally, lead from the heart. Our world, our country, our businesses, and our children, need your leadership. From the bottom of my heart, thank you all for taking your valuable time to read this book. I wish you and yours God's blessings, peace, and prosperity.

APPENDIX

A *LEAD WITH MERCY* ASSESSMENT

This is a simple assessment, summarizing many of the questions posed in the book, to give you a sense of how merciful a leader you are.* This is not a judgment of whether you are a good or a bad leader. Rather, I intend it as an assessment of whether you are applying the tenets of the *Lead with Mercy* framework (Figure A) in your leadership style. If you are, wonderful. If not, consider evolving your leadership style to include some or all of these practices.

*   A special thanks to my friends, Todd Uterstaedt, for recommending I add this assessment, and Dr. Jeff Kuhn, for recommending the scoring scale.

Figure A. Lead With Mercy Framework.

Defining M ercy

E arn the Right to Lead

R esponsibility

C larity of Vision

Lead From Y our Heart

Earning the right to lead

1. Do I lead by example in exemplifying the standards (e.g. core values, ethical standards, regulatory requirements, policies) of my organization?

2. Do I share the pain when making a difficult corporate decision (e.g. salary reductions, compensation freezes, eliminating perquisites or benefits)?

3. Do I treat my colleagues the way I want to be treated (with respect and dignity)?

4. Especially when making difficult decisions, do I consider the implications to others in my organization?

5. Do I lead with integrity in actions and deeds?

Being a responsible and accountable leader

1. Do I take ultimate responsibility when someone on my team makes a mistake or falls short?

2. Do I invest time and other resources in the development of the people I lead?

3. Do I trust my colleagues to execute their duties?

4. Do I say "we" when talking about the successes of "my" team?

5. Do I offer a sincere apology when I make a mistake?

Providing clear vision

1. Have I shared my aspirations for the team or organization?

2. Do I know to what those I lead aspire?

3. Are my team members able to articulate our vision?

4. Are my people and my organization prepared to succeed?

5. Do I focus primarily on short-terms gains, or long-term results?

Leading from the heart

1. Do I say thank you for a job well done, or congratulate people for professional or personal successes and milestones?

2. Do I know my team members (e.g. strengths, families, hobbies, passions)?

3. Do I encourage my colleagues to give back to the community?

4. Do my team members know what I and the organization expect of them professionally?

5. Am I committed to helping a struggling employee succeed, or helping a top performer make it to the next level?

Give yourself one point for every question to which to you answered yes (so you have an overall score between 0 and 20). Again, this is not a judgment of your leadership style, but rather a tool to assess whether you apply the tenets of merciful leadership. If your score is high, that is wonderful. If it is low, take some time to consider whether applying any of these tenets might further develop your leadership style.

0 - 6 points: Consider whether applying the tenets of leading with mercy might further develop your leadership style

7 - 13 points: Keep it up – and why not work to answer a few more of these questions in the affirmative?

14 - 20 points: Wonderful! Maybe you should have written this book.

✳ ✳ ✳ ✳

"People are often unreasonable and self-centered. Forgive them anyway.

If you are kind, people may accuse you of ulterior motives. Be kind anyway.

If you are honest, people may cheat you. Be honest anyway.

If you find happiness, people may be jealous. Be happy anyway.

The good you do today may be forgotten tomorrow. Do good anyway.

Give the world the best you have and it may never be enough. Give your best anyway.

For you see, in the end, it is between you and God. It was never between you and them anyway."

Blessed Mother Teresa of Calcutta

ACKNOWLEDGMENTS

I never really imagined myself as someone who would write a book, even a short one like this. The task was daunting to me, and one that required a lot of patience and perseverance. I don't necessarily have much of either – so knowing that, you can imagine a lot of people helped me get to this point – not only in writing the manuscript, but in gaining the knowledge and experience I drew upon in writing it. And indeed a lot of people did.

Before I start saying thank you, I want to share a quick story about why sharing my appreciation is so important to me. As a young man my only desire was to be an officer in the U.S. Army. I had to overcome some obstacles, primarily a medical condition that the military deemed a disqualification for commissioning as an officer. After several attempts to obtain a medical waiver were denied, I gave up hope. Fortunately, several others did not. I had a chance to say thank you to all of them except one. When the opportunity presented itself, I was too intimidated and embarrassed to express my gratitude. Several months later I learned that person passed away. I remember to this day my first reaction being that I never said thank you. I vowed to never let that happen again … I try my best to this day, to express my appreciation and my love to as many people as possible.

My wife started nudging me to write a book about a year before I actually wrote *Lead with Mercy*. I talk with her a lot about my feelings regarding the power of leadership and the importance of devoting time to your people. As I reflect back on my time in the military and the business world, it is the times I am engaging with people about their potential that I feel most energized. So my wife said, "You should write a book about it." And so I have. She has been a constructive critic and great supporter, keeping me going when I lost focus. She is an incredible woman – a faithful Christian, loving and nurturing mother, and a most patient wife.

About the time my wife suggested I write a book, my father-in-law did the same. They claim no collusion. He is a successful businessperson with a reputation for common sense, taking care of his people, and turning around failing businesses. He and I have great conversations about the power of good, strong leadership. I thank him for the inspiration and encouragement.

I've had the good fortune of having many merciful, compassionate and strong, effective leaders as bosses and mentors in the military and business world: Vice Admiral (USN, Retired) Mike McConnell, Lieutenant General (USA, Retired) Bob Noonan, Major General (USAF, Retired) Stan Musser, Colonel (USA, Retired) Bob Brown, Colonel (USA, Retired) Bill Marvin, Colonel (USA, Retired) Jim Gibbons, Colonel (USA, Retired) Jeff Rapp, Colonel (USA, Retired) Ed Schwabe, Colonel (USA, Retired) Gene Wilson, Lieutenant Colonel (USA, Retired) Doug Farris, Lieutenant Colonel (USAR, Retired) Scott Keefer, Lieutenant Colonel (USA, Retired) Bruce Lavell, Lieutenant Colonel (Retired) Mike Oriet, Lieutenant Colonel (Retired) Dave Renaud, Fred Blackburn, Dave

Carmichael, Christopher Ling, Doug Purvance, and Joanne Yuvanc. Despite my best efforts, I'm sure I've forgotten some, and I'm truly sorry for that. I'm grateful to them for leading by example and nurturing me in the days when my reserved style was seen by some as more of an obstacle to my success rather than an enabler of it. They helped me strike the balance of strengthening my leadership and communication styles while remaining authentic. They invested time and other resources in me and I am very thankful to all of them. Several of them also encouraged my efforts to write this book.

Thanks to several non-commissioned officers that guided me as a cadet and officer, including First Sergeants Sheree Kelly and Kurt Strickland; and Sergeant Major (USA, Retired) Frank Longrie and Sergeant First Class (USA, Retired) Jerry Thalison.

My leadership practices are still a work in progress, but any positive traits I have, I owe to those who granted me the right to lead and learn even when I didn't deserve it, including my soldiers and direct reports from my firm.

My father didn't know anything about this book until I was well into writing it. What he did, however, was provide me one of the first examples I can remember of leading with mercy. When I was 12 or 13, my family lived in Germany. My father was a Sergeant First Class stationed in Augsburg with the U.S. Army. During our time in Germany one of his soldiers passed away after suffering a heart attack during physical training. I remember my Dad (and Mom) devoting a lot of time to the soldier's wife and family. They lived two large apartment complexes from us in a sprawling military housing community. My dad rigged up a military field telephone (a landline) between our apartment and the soldier's apartment, so that the

+ 67 +

widow could reach us immediately day or night (call waiting didn't exist yet, let alone mobile phones for the average person). The experience is for me one that I often recall when I think about the power of compassionate leadership.

Thank you to all who have accompanied me on my journey of faith. That journey has influenced my leadership perspectives greatly. Along the way I've encountered wonderful examples of faith including military chaplains, priests, and deacons. They include Fr. and U.S. Navy Reserve Chaplain Daniel Mode, Fr. Jonathon O'Donahue, Fr. Keith O'Hare, Fr. Carroll Oubre, Fr. Peter Okola, Fr. James Searby, and Fr. Christopher Vaccaro; the "Airborne Chaplain," and Polish Army chaplain in Afghanistan whose names I just cannot recall. Just as powerful have been the examples set by the laity, as we call them, countless people who haven't been called to a religious vocation but set a wonderful example of faith, charity, and mercy in their own vocations. These people all influenced my perspectives on life and leadership. Some of them, including Jeff Kuhn and Todd Uterstaedt, directly influenced the content of this book by offering thoughtful review and critique.

Thanks to Andrew Neitlich of the Center for Executive Coaching, whose great training and mentoring in executive coaching gave me the confidence and inspiration to take action and write this book.

Finally, thanks to you – the reader – for investing your time and money in this book. I hope it has affirmed previously held perspectives or inspired new ones.

ENDNOTES

1   Gethim, R. (1998). *The Foundations of Buddhism*. Oxford University Press.

2   Peltier, B. (2010). *The Psychology of Executive Coaching: Theory and Application (2nd Edition)*. Routledge (Taylor and Francis Group).

3   Weiner, J (2012). "Managing Compassionately." Available at https://www.linkedin.com/today/post/article/20121015034012-22330283-managing-compassionately

4   Fryer, B. (2013). "The Rise of Compassionate Management (Finally)." Available at http://blogs.hbr.org/2013/09/the-rise-of-compassionate-management-finally/

5   Schwartz, T. (2013). *Companies that Practice "Conscious Capitalism" Perform 10x Better.* Available at http://blogs.hbr.org/2013/04/companies-that-practice-conscious-capitalism-perform/

6   Zeitz, J. and Grün, A. (2010). *The Manager and The Monk: A Discourse on Prayer, Profit, and Principles.* Jossey-Bass.

7   Ibid.

8   Beamer F. and Snook J. (2013). *Let Me Be Frank: My Life at Virginia Tech."* Triumph Books.

9   Widmer, A. (2011). *The Pope and the CEO.* Emmaus Road Publishing.

10   Tan, Chade-Meng (2014). *Search Inside Yourself: The Unexpected Path to Achieving Success, Happiness (and World Peace).* HarperCollins Publishers.

11   Quinn, R. and Quinn R. (2009). *Lift: Becoming a Positive Force in Any Situation.* Berrett-Kohler Publishers, Inc.

12   Ibid.

13   Peltier (2010). *The Psychology of Executive Coaching: Theory and Application (2nd Edition).*

14   Tan (2014). *Search Inside Yourself: The Unexpected Path to Achieving Success, Happiness (and World Peace).*

15   Schutz, E. (2009). "Trust and the Bottom Line: How Does Paying Attention to the Human Element in Business Improve Your Bottom Line?" The Schutz Company. Available at http://thehumanelement.com/index.php/case-studies-articles

16   Schutz, W. (1994). *The Human Element: Productivity, Self-Esteem, and the Bottom Line.* Jossey-Bass Publishers.

17   Eblin, S. (2009). *The Next Level: What Insiders Know About Executive Success.* Davies-Black.

18   Ibid.

19   Kouzes and Posner. *The Leadership Challenge: How to Make Extraordinary Things Happen in Organizations (5th Edition).* The Leadership Challenge – A Wiley Brand.

20   Eblin. *The Next Level: What Insiders Know About Executive Success.*

21   Goldsmith, M. (2007). *What Got You Here Won't Get You There: How Successful People Become Even More Successful!* Hyperion.

22   Tan (2014). *Search Inside Yourself: The Unexpected Path to Achieving Success, Happiness (and World Peace).*

23   Ibid.

24   *The Holy Bible (New American Bible), John 3:16.* Our Sunday Visitor Publishing Division.

25   Gethim (1998). *The Foundations of Buddhism.*

26   Masao, K. (2005); Clark, T. (2007). *The Swordless Samurai: Leadership Wisdom of Japan's 16th-Century Legend – Toyotomi Hideyoshi.* Truman Talley Books.

27   Goldsmith (2007). *What Got You Here Won't Get You There: How Successful People Become Even More Successful!*

28   Engel B. (2002). "The Power of Apology." Available at http://www.psychologytoday.com/articles/200208/the-power-apology

29   Schwartz, T. (2014). "You Don't Have to Hate Your Job." *New York Times online, accessed June 11, 2014.*

30   Neitlich, A. (2001). *Elegant Leadership.*

31 Kouzes and Posner. *The Leadership Challenge: How to Make Extraordinary Things Happen in Organizations (5ᵗʰ Edition).*

32 Katherine Hyatt, *"The Influence of Vision on Perceived Organizational Support,"* Kravis Leadership Institute, Leadership Review, Vol. 11, Spring 2011, pp. 157-170.

33 McChrystal, S. (2013). *My Share of the Task: A Memoir.* The Penguin Group.

34 Joint Publication 1-02 (2010 amended 2014). *Department of Defense Dictionary and Associated Terms.*

35 Turak A. (2013). *Business Secrets of the Trappist Monks: One CEO's Quest for Meaning and Authenticity.* Columbia Business School Publishing.

36 Knox, N. (2005). *USA Today online, accessed June 25, 2014.*

37 Turak (2013). *Business Secrets of the Trappist Monks: One CEO's Quest for Meaning and Authenticity.*

38 Kouzes and Posner. *The Leadership Challenge: How to Make Extraordinary Things Happen in Organizations (5ᵗʰ Edition).*

39 Ibid.

40 http://christianity.about.com/od/glossary/a/Agape.htm accessed September 8, 2014

41 Greenleaf, R. (1970). *The Servant As Leader (2008 reprint).* The Greenleaf Center for Servant Leadership.

42 Schwartz. "You Don't Have to Hate Your Job." *New York Times online, accessed June 11, 2014.*

ENDNOTES

43   www.army.mil/features/ShinsekiFarewell/farewellremarks.htm accessed August 6, 2014.

44   Interview with Robert W. Noonan, Jr., Lieutenant General, U.S. Army (Retired), August 5, 2014.

45   Kaye, B. and Jordan-Evans, S. (2008). *Love 'Em or Lose 'Em: Getting Good People to Stay – 26 Engagement Strategies for Busy Managers.* Berrett-Kohler Publishers.

46   "2011 Executive Summary: Deloitte Volunteer IMPACT Survey (2011). Available at http://www.deloitte.com/assets/Dcom-UnitedStates/Local%20Assets/Documents/us_2011DeloitteVolunteerIMPACTSurvey_ExecutiveSummary_060311.pdf, accessed June 27, 2014.

47   www.giveanhour.org accessed June 27, 2014.

48   Goldsmith (2007). *What Got You Here Won't Get You There: How Successful People Become Even More Successful!*

49   Schutz (2009). "Trust and the Bottom Line: How Does Paying Attention to the Human Element in Business Improve Your Bottom Line?" Available at http://thehumanelement.com/index.php/case-studies-articles

50   Weiner, J (2012). "Managing Compassionately." Available at https://www.linkedin.com/today/post/article/20121015034012-22330283-managing-compassionately

51   Fryer (2013). "The Rise of Compassionate Management (Finally)." Available at http://blogs.hbr.org/2013/09/the-rise-of-compassionate-management-finally/

52   Schwartz (2013). *Companies that Practice "Conscious Capitalism" Perform 10x Better.* Available at http://blogs.hbr.org/2013/04/companies-that-practice-conscious-capitalism-perform/

53   Ibid.

54   Williams (2012). "Why We Need Kind and Compassionate Leaders: Kindness, Compassion, and Empathy Will Change Toxic Workplaces." Available at http://www.psychologytoday.com/blog/wired-success/201208/why-we-need-kind-and-compassionate-leaders

55   Tan (2014). *Search Inside Yourself: The Unexpected Path to Achieving Success, Happiness (and World Peace).*

56   about.zappos.com accessed August 13, 2014.

57   Hsieh, T. (2010). *Delivering Happiness: A Path to Profits, Passion, and Purpose.* Business Plus, Hachette Book Group, Inc.

CPSIA information can be obtained at www.ICGtesting.com
Printed in the USA
BVOW01s1244240315

393041BV00001B/33/P